GARISH
GARDENS
OUTLANDISH
LAWNS

GARISH GARDENS OUTLANDISH LAWNS

RONALD C. MODRA
M. B. ROBERTS

WILLOW CREEK PRESS
Minocqua, Wisconsin

Willow Creek Press
P.O. Box 147 • Minocqua, Wisconsin 54548

For information on
other Willow Creek titles,
call 1-800-850-9453

**Library of Congress
Cataloging-in-Publication Data**

Modra, Ronald C.
    Garish Gardens, outlandish lawns / Ronald
C. Modra, M.B. Roberts.
        p.   cm.
    ISBN 1-57223-140-8
    1. Garden ornaments and furniture--United
States.   I. Roberts, M.B. (Mary Beth) II. Title.
    SB473.5.M641998
    717--dc21   98-10115
                                CIP

Printed in Canada

DEDICATION

For Ronnie — MB Roberts
For MB — Ron Modra

ACKNOWLEDGMENTS

Thanks to Tom Petrie and Heather, and all the Willow Creek gang for their work and input on this book. Thanks to Pat and Sue Jordan, for their help and understanding. Thanks to my mom and especially Pop, for his sense of humor and for finding the flamingo king! And to others who contributed time and helped us find garish treasures, especially Jodi Siewart, Paul "Bubb" Schiraldi, Kelly and Dolores Modra, John Beda, Lauranne Poupart, Steve Duba, George Hunker, Alberto Colonia, Mike Sipe, Sherri and Simon Dearden-Hose, Richard Stanczyk, M.B. and Eileen Sullivan, Margaret Townsend, Ken Akers, Manda Roberts and Bruce Miller. Thanks also to Tom Hamburg for his continuous help and inspiration. And most of all, thanks to all the outrageous and creative gardeners who welcomed us into their homes and let us photograph their yards. This is for you.

TABLE OF CONTENTS

SHIP OUT OF WATER   *Here's one trusty old tub, belonging to a fisherman/gardener from Ashland, Wisconsin, that was saved from the trash heap by a cluster of wildflowers.*

AUTHOR'S NOTE

THIS LAND IS OUTLANDISH

I grew up in Vienna, Virginia, a suburb of Washington, DC, where spring, summer and fall weekends were spent washing the car and mowing the lawn. The yards in our neighborhood were pretty unremarkable. Pretty, but unremarkable.

Almost every yard in our neighborhood boasted a half-acre of green, lush grass with several grand oaks and a smattering of evergreens. Several symmetrical green bushes grew beneath the first-floor windows of each partially brick, partially aluminum-sided house. Maybe a dogwood tree and a couple of azalea bushes would be planted out front for a splash of color in the spring. Oh, and the daffodils. They were spectacular in their proud yellow rows for two weeks every April.

The well-cared-for, not-quite-elegant yards in our neighborhood were almost entirely interchangeable, especially the fronts. No written rules in our development defined how the yards and homes should look. We had no block association to create or enforce any potential mandates. With the exception of the time Mr. Wilson, who never said much to anyone, told my best friend's father, "Hey, Ted! You've got bagworms!", it was rare that one neighbor would make a negative comment directly to another.

LEFT   *A plastic classic.*

The pressure to keep the yard nice (and bagworm-free) was usually more of the keep-up-with-the-Joneses, subtle, variety. Every Saturday morning, dads, and sometimes moms, were working in the yard. Raking leaves. Edging the sidewalks. Being good Americans. All was normal. And tidy.

It was not until I went to college, at Virginia Tech in Blacksburg, Virginia, that I first saw communities where the lawns weren't manicured and the gardens weren't entirely comprised of things you plant. Driving from northern Virginia to school in Blacksburg, at the southwestern tip of the state, I passed through small towns, mountain towns and in some cases poor towns where what people lacked in money they often made up for in ingenuity. They made a little bridge out of wood planks to cover a ditch. They planted flowers in old tractor tires painted white. Or they stuck pussy willows pulled from alongside the creek into glass jugs that were placed on either side of a front walkway to greet visitors in a fashion loosely reminiscent of the stone lions which are often seen on both sides of a mansion's gate.

Some of the yard accessories, especially the wooden, handmade kind were cute, I thought. Some, especially the plastic, store-bought variety, I thought . . . were not. It's a matter of opinion. A matter of taste. One thing I did know for sure: it was fun to drive down a street that featured outlandish lawns. Discovering them made me want to get off the interstate and take back roads so that I would see every one.

What kind of people place metal cut-out characters in positions at various points on their lawns so they appear to be having a conversation? Who lives in the house by the lake where the front and back yards are carpeted with animal statues, old mailboxes, and year-round Christmas decorations?

I am lucky. I got a chance to find out the answers to these questions with Ron Modra, my incredibly talented partner (who recently became my husband). At first Ron, a sports photographer, was skeptical. Typically, he spent his days photographing game action or doing portraits of athletes, often

A Minocqua, Wisconsin menagerie.

famous ones. It was difficult for him to make the leap to plastic, inanimate objects. But after a particularly humiliating first day, when a crowd gathered around him as he lay on his stomach in someone's yard photographing a row of toilets with geraniums protruding from the bowls, he was over the hump.

He actually became enthusiastic as he saw how cooperative the gardeners were whom we approached to photograph. Also, Ron had just purchased a large-format camera, which we affectionately and reverently call "Mr. Fuji," which lent itself to the type of "beauty" photographs he wanted to do.

We began to really enjoy our adventure through Americana. We quickly realized we were barely scratching the surface of the creative ways people express themselves in this country.

To all the garish gardeners we met, we thank you and dedicate this book to you. This book is also for those people who would never dare put something strange in their yard but who delight in those who do.

ON THE ROAD

Honey, did you see that yard ball?" I said, as our rented blue Grand Am whizzed past an Ohio farm house.

"No, honey," Ronnie answered through gritted teeth. "I'm trying to drive."

His hands tightly gripped the steering wheel as we drove down the two-lane county road with huge 18-wheelers speeding in our direction, separated from us by nothing more than a painted yellow line.

I calculated his anxiety level. High. But we didn't have one single picture of a yard ball yet. I wanted one. I decided to push it.

"Well, it was a good one," I said. "Really good."

We had been arguing about yard balls all day. I would call out when I saw one, usually asking if he saw it. He usually said, no, he was trying to drive. It bothered me when we passed by things. I feared we would never see anything just like it again.

Ronnie pulled onto the road's shoulder.

"I hope this one is really good," he sighed.

"It is," I said.

He executed a three-point turn and headed back three miles in the direction from which we had just come. We turned into the long driveway of the farm house I had spotted. The sprawling lawn was mowed short. All the trees, bushes and plants were robust but neatly clipped.

Smack in the front was my yard ball, an oversized shiny red sphere resting on a stand surrounded by a mound of red and white impatiens. We parked next to the house and I went to knock on the screen door. A fortyish woman answered the door, with a friendly but quizzical, "Yes?"

"Hi," I said. "I'm sorry to bother you. We're working on a book about gardens and lawns . . ."

"Oh! Well, you'll need to see this," she said stepping past me and walking toward the backyard. I looked over my shoulder and gave the "thumbs up" to Ronnie, who began to unload his camera equipment from the back seat.

"These weathervanes, my father made," she said, gesturing toward a row of 2-dimensional roosters placed evenly along the top of a log post fence. She showed me around the barn where outside there were two wooden wagons full of pots of blue petunias. She continued her tour. I spotted several fluorescent, plastic spirals she had hanging from the lowest branches of a maple tree.

"What do you call those?" I asked.

"Oh, I don't know," she smiled. "I just like them."

When we began this project, we wondered if it would be difficult getting strangers to let us take their photographs. We guessed that about half the people we approached would say "No thanks," if not "Go away."

We were absolutely wrong.

Of the approximately fifty people we approached to be in this book, only one person turned us down: our next-door neighbor who declined to be photographed in her curlers and housecoat.

We were surprised to learn something that now seems so obvious. Anyone who goes to the effort of dragging a four-foot, 150-pound, manatee mailbox to their curb (and puts a cowboy hat on its head) is making a statement. These touches aren't just for themselves. They're for us. The passers-by. Garish gardeners want us to stop and look. And talk. They're the type of people who will invite you in when you pull into their driveway in your rented blue Grand Am.

We took the bulk of the pictures for this book driving from Connecticut to Wisconsin. Each time we got out of the car to meet someone new was a delight. We enjoyed meeting people. Even more, we enjoyed simply getting out of the car.

"I want that yard," I'd say. "I want to talk to the guy standing outside."

"But there's no light in that yard," he'd say.

"I thought you were supposed to be such a good photographer," I'd scowl.

I am compulsive, too much a reporter. I wanted to get a picture of every yard, see everything. So much that I was dreaming of pink flamingoes and getting vertigo from seeing whirligigs in my sleep. It was only when I saw the developed film of the above-mentioned red yard ball did I realize I needed to trust my photographer. He was right. We didn't need a photo of every yard ball in America. We just needed one great one.

I think we got it.

AUTHOR'S NOTE

GARDEN REFLECTIONS   *The quintessential yard ball does its Crestline, Ohio garden proud.*

THE FLAMINGO KING
The Man Who Started It All

"Before plastics, only rich people could afford to have poor taste." —Donald Featherstone

*P*icture yourself as a contestant on the old *Password* television game show. You are receiving clues. Your partner whispers: "Tacky . . ."

You think you know the answer but you hesitate. Then your partner slowly enunciates another clue, "Plastic . . ."

"Pink flamingo!" you shout, winning the game.

Tacky goes with pink plastic yard flamingo like butter goes with popcorn. Since its introduction in 1957, the pink plastic bird has evolved into the icon of lawn ornaments.

Why do we love them so? Union Products, a plastics manufacturer in Leominster, Massachusetts, sells about a half a million each year. Between 15 and 20 million have been sold since they were introduced. Surely some of us are buying them as a joke.

To "flamingo" someone's yard, perhaps? But the rest of us must like them. It's simple mathematics.

LEFT *Donald Featherstone, creator of the pink plastic lawn flamingo, with his personal 40-strong flock.*

ABOVE *A wooden pelican hand-crafted in Pelican Lake, Wisconsin.*

RIGHT *This South Bend, Indiana geese quartet (kept from flying away by the sand in their bottoms) were a gift from a husband whose wife was depressed after her real geese were killed by a weasel. They cheer her every day.*

As to the pink flamingo's longevity, Nancy Featherstone has a theory: "It's good design," she says. "You can't argue with that."

Nancy is married to Donald Featherstone, the man who created the pink plastic yard flamingo.

"Imagine telling other wives that at cocktail parties," she says.

Her husband is a tall, affable man with a businessman's parted-on-the-side haircut. He has an easy smile and quick chuckle. In 1957, he graduated from The School of the Worcester Art Museum then immediately got a job with Union Products, the only place he has ever worked. The flamingo was his second assignment.

"I made a duck first," he says, "which actually sells more."

But of course it was the flamingo which put the proverbial "feather" in his "stone." He originally sculpted the flamingo out of clay, borrowing poses from the famous "flock of flamingos" *National*

Geographic photograph. There already were 2-D flamingos made of plywood on the market, Featherstone says. Then a foam version came out, but dogs tended to eat them. So his flamingo, actually flamingos (there are two poses, "up neck" and "down neck" which are sold in pairs) evolved.

His original model had wooden dowels for legs, but Featherstone says they were too expensive to make and plastic wasn't strong enough. Hence, metal rod legs became the standard. Union Products later tried to again produce and market a deluxe model with wooden yellow legs, which Featherstone says looked very natural, but it didn't sell. The now classic metal legs remain.

The flamingo body is made of durable plastic. "The same stuff they ship acid and glue in," Featherstone says.

This material is not reserved for flamingos only. Union Products, which Featherstone bought from the former owners in 1996, manufactures a line of some 800 products. Featherstone sculpted every one of them.

ABOVE It's a Jungle Out There! *In Key West, Florida, if garish gardeners neglect their yards for even a week, it's machete time.*

LEFT *Paul "Bubb" Schiraldi, from The Bronx, New York, takes a break from riding his Harley to do a little lawn duty the morning before his daughter, Alexandra Paul, is christened.*

Featherstone has many of his creations on display on his own property. The front yard is surprisingly simple, the only adornments being a couple neat rows of marigolds and two gray plastic chickens that sit on their haunches like the stone lions that well-to-do people often have guarding their entranceways.

"Before plastics," Featherstone says stepping past the chickens, "only rich people could afford to have poor taste."

He walks into the tiny, shaded, fenced-in back-yard which is mostly made up of a driveway and a garage. Next to the driveway is a small swatch of grass, which is the width and about half the length of a bowling lane. On the grass is a cluster of forty Donald Featherstone signature flamingos. "I sign them, like Calvin Klein," he says of the raised plastic autograph stamped onto each flamingo belly.

LEFT *More from the Featherstone farm.*

ABOVE *Some of Featherstone's flock relocated to Florida.*

Along the chainlink fence stands the flamingos' supporting cast. There is a rooster and a hen with three chicks. There is a mama duck with three baby ducks "walking" behind her. There is a frog. A deer family. A pink and gray elephant. A squirrel. A bear, sheep, pig and cow. Two cartoonish crows which Featherstone insists are not "Heckle and Jeckle." A fire hydrant. A parking meter. An Uncle Sam and a white yard jockey with a mustard-colored coat. All plastic, of course. A veritable Union Products catalog. Live and on parade.

It seems the Featherstones don't mind a bit of attention. They are used to it. Stories profiling Donald and his flamingo, which celebrated its fortieth anniversary in 1997, have appeared on television and in daily newspapers all over the country, as well as in *The National Enquirer*.

It is easy to understand why the Featherstones don't mind the media attention: each story results in flamingos flying off the shelves, two-by-two. They are also good-natured about the ribbing they inevitably receive.

"As long as they keep buying them, I really don't care," Featherstone says.

At least once a week he hears a story such as the one about the woman in Centreville, Maryland who has a flock of 34 Featherstone flamingos that she constantly dresses and rearranges in different situations, such as a nativity scene at Christmas. Or the one about the car dealership in Oklahoma that started a publicity campaign by blanketing random yards with flamingos in the middle of the night. It all tickles him.

Featherstone says he is satisfied that he did something in his life that amuses people. Beyond that he is proud to have created an instantly identifiable American icon, rivaled only by maybe Marilyn Monroe's face or a classic Coca-Cola bottle. It's inspiring. Featherstone is back to work. His next creation: an ostrich.

Surely, it will be a fine bird. But it's no flamingo.

ABOVE   *Fort Lauderdale, Florida has the highest number of yard flamingos per capita in the continental United States.*

Fat Elvis and pink flamingos go together like peas and carrots.

A young bride is sitting at the head table during her wedding reception. Several guests tap their forks against their water glasses. When the dinging becomes deafening, the bride and groom kiss. Applause.

The bride notices that the d.j. has stopped playing music. Then she hears someone singing, "I'm caught in a trap . . . I can't hold back . . ." It sounds like Elvis. She whips her veiled head around and is startled to find herself being serenaded by a huge man who resembles Elvis at his tackiest.

The Elvis look-alike leans over close to her face. He picks up her fork and begins eating off her plate.

The crowd bursts into laughter. The bride laughs and kisses the crooner. Again, applause.

On closer examination, the bride can see that the Elvis is in fact the d.j., Mike Sipe, who has changed into a custom-made fat suit, complete with glittery cape and topped off with glasses and sideburns. This is his alter-ego, "Pelvis," a character he created in 1995.

"I've always loved Elvis," said Sipe, a serious Elvis fan. He claims it was after he moved to South Florida that the idea for Pelvis came to him.

"I've seen everybody do Elvis," he said. "I didn't want to make fun of him but at the same time I wanted to do something tongue-in-cheek."

When Sipe saw a guy in a fat suit at a costume party, he got the inspiration for Pelvis. Now he is booked at more weddings and corporate parties than he can count. He even played the Tropicana in Las Vegas recently. A personal thrill.

Sipe says back home in Indiana, he had a garden where his favorite thing was the sweet corn that grew there. Sipe, who is busy running his entertainment company of 42 employees who range from straight-away d.j.'s to Polynesian dancers, doesn't have much of a garden in Florida. He claims he has no pink flamingos in his own garden.

"But Pelvis does," he said.

Thank you very much.

Wood is natural. Real. Solid. Beautiful. Something to mold, hand-craft and paint.

In gardens, wood is normally perceived as a gentrified material. The stuff with which white picket fences are made. Country-style, hand-painted "Welcome" signs are made from wood.

Some followers of garden kitsch have noticed an apparent shift in taste. There has been an increase in peer pressure that garden ornaments should be hand-made from organic materials.

This is ironic given the annual rise in the sale of plastic garden creatures. It is doubly ironic that the first, pre-plastic lawn flamingos were 2-dimensional and made of wood.

Still, even if "wood is good," it's a matter of taste.

CUT IT OUT *2-D decor is all the rage in many Michigan (top) and Indiana (bottom) yards.*

FAR RIGHT *This whimsical wood cut-out graces a triangular lot at a New Castle, Pennsylvania intersection.*

LEFT *Carol Eberly of South Whitley, Indiana, who owns Carol's Drive-in, keeps two wooden cows in the back yard of her home next door. She made them after spotting two similar cows on a long drive (she drives a truck in the winter when the drive-in is closed). She pulled her semi over to the side of the road, snapped a picture of the originals, then cut out and painted her own pair upon returning home.*

Some kids tried to steal them once but Carol caught them as they struggled to fit one of the heifers into their car. Carol's glad they didn't make off with her bovine pair. They seem to help the drive-in business. "People see them and want ice cream," she laughs.

ABOVE *Peeping from the evergreens in Boulder Junction, Wisconsin.*

TOP LEFT *Every day's a holiday in Oceola, Ohio.*

WHIRLIGIGS, WEATHERVANES, WINDMILLS, WHATNOTS

*D*onald's Duck Shoppe and Gallery sells weathervanes, among other things. Folks love them. It seems that as long as there has been wind people have looked for answers blowing in it. People have always been intrigued by the wind, seeking out ways to ride it or capture it. At the very least, people seem to want to know which way it's moving.

For that, we have weathervanes, which have been around almost as long as there have been barns and roofs to hold them. Weathervanes have almost always consisted of a flat piece of metal (rooster added later), placed on a roof to swing with the wind and show its path. Today, many weathervanes, usually those made of aluminum and copper, also function as lightning rods.

Contemporary weathervane designs vary. There are simple ones, an arrow with a ball might do. There are extraordinary ones, such as a polished cherub, a Model T Ford or a cow. (According to the Donald's Duck Shoppe brochure, "A cow with its tail to the west means the weather is best. A cow with its tail to the east means the weather is least.")

LEFT   *Spinning . . . not just for the birds.*

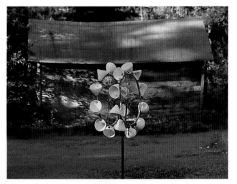

ABOVE
Clorox top what-not; Cocky: a classic barn top.

RIGHT
A Gainesville, Florida, yard waits for a cool breeze.

Where there are weathervanes, there are bound to be whirligigs. According to Wilson Woodcraft, the largest producer of whirligigs in the country, (20,000 sold annually), 'gigs are really "comic weathervanes."

They are closely related; the two have even been grouped together in an exhibit at Laumeier Park in St. Louis, "Whirligigs and Weathervanes: An exhibition of Contemporary Sculpture."

Still, the whirligig is usually considered the weathervane's less functional cousin, stuck into the ground to mindlessly whirl and spin when the wind blows. They're there for looks (if you like that kind of thing).

But give the whirligig its due. Whirligigs first became popular in New England where farmers and sawyers crafted them during their idle winter months. Country folk in the Northeast and across the U.S. originally used them to keep small critters away from crops.

Today, the plastic, primary-colored variety can be seen in gardens everywhere. Just for fun. This round, flower or pinwheel design that people pluck from

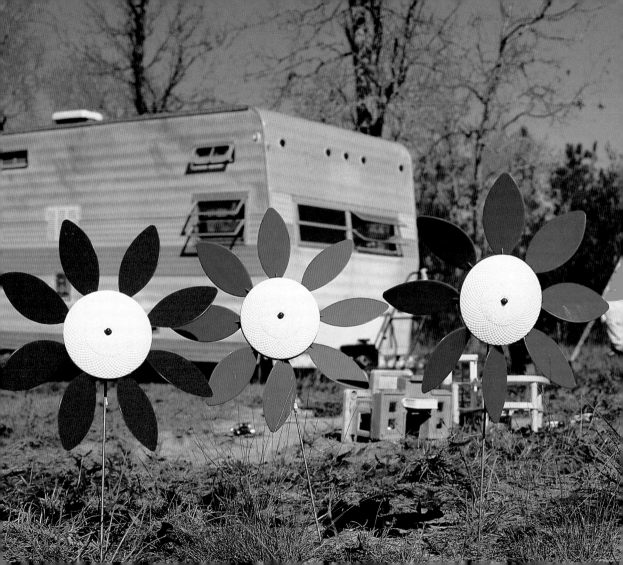

boxes in a discount store's garden section is the most popular, closely followed by plastic birds and bees. But there are a variety of whirligigs that don't just spin. They are moveable, wooden cartoons. When the wind blows, donkeys kick, a lobster boat bobs at sea or two baseball players pitch and hit. There is a whirligig golfer that putts and a whirligig man milking a cow. Making these 'gigs is an art form.

There is a man in Lucama, NC, Vollis Simpson, who is arguably the whirligig king. He made his first whirligig to power a washing machine while stationed in the Mariana Islands in WWII. After the war, he built a huge windmill that powered a heating system in his house. He then ran both a machine shop and a house-moving business, which gave him the materials and the know-how to develop his advanced whirligigs, several of which are featured in the American Visionary Museum.

He was commissioned to create four whirligigs for the 1996 Olympics in Atlanta: his "man sawing,"

ABOVE *Dick Gottfried of Upper Sandusky, Ohio, has 22 weather vanes atop his house and barn, most of which he made. The horse weather vane is made from old lamp parts.*

LEFT *A Poplar, Wisconsin artisan gets his inspiration from the recycling bin.*

"water pumper," "man on a unicycle" and a duck that weighed thousands of pounds and rose up to 400 feet.

His quest, he says, is to take abandoned industrial parts ("stuff that's too good to throw away") and create something magical from it.

Simpson is reminiscent of a certain Cervantes' character, who also had quite an imagination. Don Quixote didn't make windmills; rather, his imagination was stirred by the windmills he saw. Who knows what a garish gardener sees in the spinny things on his lawn? Maybe they know. There's magic in the wind.

TOP LEFT *Sailing in the wind, Eagle River, Wisconsin.*

BOTTOM LEFT *Some ducks, such as this Huntersville, NC mallard, never seem to get too far.*

RIGHT *Best friends Katie Reis and Hailey Sherman go Dutch in Glendale, Wisconsin.*

*T*o some people, a garden is their sanctuary. A place to escape. To others, a garden is a place where visitors are welcome. They are encouraged to come in.

Either way, a garden is always so much more than just a pretty place. There are scents to consider. And food, sometimes, in the way of vegetables and herbs. And there are sounds. Such as birds singing. Or the gentle *ribbit* of a frog. Or maybe just the simple, barely audible whirring of two AA batteries pushing a trio of plastic sunflowers through their guitar-strumming rhythms.

A pair of batteries is as essential to some gardeners as fertilizer or water. How else then will the plastic frog sitting on a stone at the foot of the walkway croak when a visitor walks past? Or how else will a plastic banjo-playing tulip offer up the soft chords of a song such as "Oh Suzannah"?

Wherever a whimsical bouncing rubber cactus is found, know that the Energizer Bunny can't be far behind.

TOP *Green duo in Cumberland, Maryland.*

BOTTOM *Soloist. He croaks when a gardener walks past.*

RIGHT *This sunny Washington, DC trio rocks and rolls every time a door slams or a dog barks.*

*S*ome people look at a wall socket and see a place to plug in a lamp. Others see a face with two eyes and a mouth open in an expression of surprise or astonishment. The latter is the sort of person who would never be stumped as to what to do with a stump.

They see it before they even take on the task of making the leftover part of a tree into something jocular. They squint, as one would when looking up and imagining clouds as dragons and castles. Then they get an idea. And decide they're never going to fit into that bathing suit anyway.

People who dress stumps are inviting passersby to stop and chuckle. And comment.

After all, they live at the beach. Their front yards are mostly sand and shells. So there's spare time for extra endeavors. Such as dressing up stumps.

LEFT *Just another pretty face, Key Largo, Florida.*
RIGHT *Stumped in Key Largo.*

WHAT TO DO
WITH THAT OLD TOILET

*F*or centuries, people have been bringing the outside *in*. Since the invention of the dining room table, no tulip has been safe from becoming the splash of color in a centerpiece. Baby's breath and ferns are more likely to stand up and begin jumping rope than they are to complete their life cycle outside, still in the ground.

But a different sort of phenomenon has been evolving in many garish gardens across the country. Some people, it seems, are bringing the inside *out*.

It is a fact of modern life that our appliances and bathroom receptacles eventually wear out and need to be replaced. Most of us give little thought as to what to do with that old washing machine, toilet, sink or bathtub. We usually take it to the dump, or let the Goodwill haul it away for us.

Not these garish gardeners. They wouldn't dream of wasting a perfectly good slab of porcelain. So it doesn't drain properly anymore. That doesn't mean it's *trash*. The bowl of the

LEFT   *There are pots of porcelain at the end of this rainbow in State College, Pennsylvania.*

sink or toilet is the perfect size and shape for a clump of petunias. And just imagine how many trays of impatiens a bathtub will hold. Their very non-function is the art of it.

They've turned their gardens inside out.

TOP LEFT & RIGHT *Blue Mountain, Pennsylvania.*
BOTTOM RIGHT *Just add water*
FAR RIGHT *Bathroom blooms in Land O' Lakes, Wisconsin.*

WHAT TO DO WITH THAT OLD TOILET

A Fuller Brush salesman is walking down a street. He's had a bad morning. (Two no-answers, two no-thank-yous, and one slammed door). He figures the next house he visits is crucial. He needs a success, or at least a friendly encounter, or he's quitting for the day.

He sees two houses. One is surrounded by a fence with a locked gate in front. The yard is neat with one matching green bush on either side of the door. There are no flowers. The house on the other side of the street has no fence. The lawn is tidy. There are four hanging pots of impatiens hanging on the front porch over two wooden rocking chairs painted white. There is a cluster of ceramic animals around a bird bath. The driveway is lined with fourteen ceramic frogs on one side and twelve spinning primary-colored sunflowers on the other.

Which house should he approach? His gut tells him to follow the frogs. The whole front yard feels like an enormous welcome mat to the salesman. He will more than likely make a sale. But he better write-off the rest of the afternoon. He's not leaving that place any time soon.

ABOVE *George Eutzy of Carlisle, Pennsylvania has some fifteen homemade birdhouses in his backyard. He bought this rocking horse at a school surplus sale "for his grandchildren."*

RIGHT *Eutzy says these houses are more like motels. Most of his fair-weather feathered tenants head south after a brief stay.*

THE TEXAS TORNADO

*I*t has long been said that "one man's trash is another man's treasure." Anyone who has left a thrift shop having paid two dollars for a Donna Karan cashmere sweater with the tags still on it knows firsthand that this can be so.

There is a woman in Ft. Lauderdale, Florida, who not only believes in this old adage, but has adopted it as her mantra. She has single-handedly stretched the saying to the point that it may become necessary to coin an entirely new cliché. Just for her.

To 70-year-old Lera Bradley, everyone's trash is her potential treasure.

Every day she rescues at least one discarded three-legged chair from someone's dumpster, hoists it onto her shoulders and stacks it on the back of her pick-up truck. Pass by a bent, rusted curtain rod protruding from beneath the lid of a garbage bin? Never. *Something could be done with that.*

Twice a month in Victoria Park, the neighborhood where Lera lives, people put out their bulk trash items, such as old couches or toilets, for pick-up by the city. Most people drag their bruised and battered discards to the curb the night before. Nonetheless, the mornings

of Bulk Trash Day, Ft. Lauderdale city workers find their workload light. Because most of the time, Lera has beaten them to it. She has helped herself to the good stuff under the cover of night. Maybe an oven with one working burner. Or a cracked birdbath. Or tangled, mangled blinds. It all finds a home at Lera's.

Lera's red-roofed, Mediterranean style house is a lemon-yellow shrine to the spoils of her treasure hunts. It is the halfway house for the things she collects. Some of it she resells. Some of it she keeps. (To fix up or for "investment purposes.") Here, she also showcases her myriad of "organic things."

"Come on. I'll show you my plants," she says. "This Chinese one is worth something."

The "Chinese one" grows alongside a wooden cane which had been thrust deep into the dirt. There is a twisted cactus with a rusty bike chain wrapped around its trunk. There are all manner of cacti, at least twenty or thirty, all in their own pots, ready for quick relocation. Lera has an orange tree, ficus bushes and queen palms. There are red sisters, aloe plants and clusters of elephant grass. And plastic milk crates full of shells. And another crate full of different plastic containers.

"One of my neighbors says I have too many plants," she said, handing the visitor a cutting from a prickly pear. "How can you have too many plants? They get after me for having too many yard sales, too."

Lera continued the tour by showing off two chipped wrought iron garden stools which she had converted to tables by topping them with slabs of marble. Nearby, a six-foot stuffed Ninja Turtle sat on a plastic chaise lawn chair below a "Crime Watch Area" sign. A homemade "for sale" sign was taped on an oily four-foot square metal box with a three-foot round hole in one side. Nearby was a Roman-style statue of a woman who was hoisting a water jug over her head, which caused her toga to slip.

Lera hopped up on a stone garden bench, motioning for a newly arrived visitor to join her. She and Lera looked over the fence together into her neighbor's tidy,

ABOVE *Lera welcomes a visitor to her Fort Lauderdale, Florida home.*

LEFT (BOTH) *"How can you have too many plants?" Lera asked, pointing to her "chinese one" and the supporting cast.*

ABOVE *One woman's treasures.*

sparse yard. The grass was perfectly mowed and edged. A few small bushes were planted in neat, measured rows against the freshly painted mango house.

"He's the one who calls [the city] on me," she said. "One time I put some of my trash in his bin. Now he parks it way down . . ."

"Want anything from the store, Von?" a guest staying with Lera asked.

After he left, the visitor asked why the houseguest called her "Von."

"Oh, that's my stage name," she said, picking up a cord from a gold-plated space heater. "Von Ray, the Texas Tornado. I was a stripper in New Orleans. Famous, too."

She had a scrapbook to prove it. The Texas Tornado was the operator of the Torch Club on Bourbon Street. She brought out decades-old publicity pictures, some bizarre (her half-man, half-woman act), some simply gorgeous. Movie star, perfect figure, long red hair, long eyelashes, gorgeous. I flipped to a glossy photo of Von standing on her head wearing nothing but a feather boa.

"I can still do that," she said.

She flipped to a picture of Von Ray in a bikini. It was obvious that she was the woman in the pictures. Minus a few years of gravity, she still had a good figure.

"What do you eat?" the visitor asked.

"For breakfast? Raw garlic. Sausage. Eggs. Cheese," she counted on her fingers. "Then for dinner, whatever I want. I stay busy."

Then, without warning, she put her palms on the pavement and put her knees on her elbows. She extended her legs up straight and pointed her toes. A perfect headstand.

"I'm a businesswoman," she said, shaking slightly but still holding the pose. "First and foremost."

"Well, I'd better not keep you any longer," the visitor said to Lera, whose face was flushed.

Lera brought her legs down, lifted herself upright and exhaled loudly.

"You come by anytime," she told the visitor. "Come tomorrow. I'll have some new things."

Then the visitor remembered. It was Monday afternoon. Followed by Monday night. The night when people put out their bulk trash. Treasure.

LEFT *"I'm a business woman," Lera said. The upright statue to her left may or may not be for sale.*

RIGHT *Coffee grounds make excellent fertilizer.*

THE TEXAS TORNADO

*C*ars. We love them. Live in them. Many of us become quite attached to them. And anyone who has ever been around a fisherman knows how he feels about his boat. Most would sleep in them if given the chance.

And bikers. Forget about it. A motorcycle becomes a biker's appendage. More than just his mode of transport. It is a part of him.

So what happens when cars no longer start and have to be parked, when boats begin to leak and have to be docked and when a motorcycle's parts come loose and fall to the highway with a clank?

Sometimes these cars, boats and parts are simply brought home. Given refuge in the yard by a visionary gardener who doesn't look at a rusty pipe and see just a rusty pipe. The visionaries see potential. A pipe that is half-empty could soon be half-full of flowers. See the pipe no more. It's a Zen thing. It's all a part of maintenance. Bikers, boaters and car owners are used to that.

ABOVE *Out of gas in Lac du Flambeau, Wisconsin.*

RIGHT *Parked: What inspired this State College, Pennsylvania homeowner to plant the front end of this VW so it would appear to be exploding out of the ground? What happened to the back end?*

HEY, I COULD MAKE A PLANTER OUT OF THAT!

A rose is a rose is a rose. Even an artificial one? The answer would have to be yes. As anyone with any sense of style knows, it's not the daffodil but what one does with it.

A flower stuck in the right place in just the right way gets a lot of play. In the movies, a detective is told to look for the man wearing the red carnation on his lapel. A man falls in love at first sight with a woman wearing a single gardenia in her hair. A young lover doing the tango holds a single rose in his teeth. Dramatic scenes, all.

Certain inanimate objects beg to have a flower stuck inside them. The flower then stays.

Say it with flowers and say no more.

LEFT *Long-time Harley Davidson enthusiast Steve Duba found the perfect flower pots in two discarded Harley "heads." His arrangements are proudly displayed at his biker/family-friendly pub, The Boulder Beer Bar in Boulder Junction, Wisconsin.*

ABOVE *Jerry North, owner of the "Holiday House" in Glendale, Wisconsin is the proud owner of an antique washing machine.*

RIGHT *They made their beds . . .*

"AM I SUFFICIENTLY INSANE?"

A man takes an old brass headboard and drives it in the ground. Then he plants flowers in a rectangle configuration in front of the headboard. Voilà. "A flower bed."

Who would do such a thing? Quite a few people, as it turns out.

There is a retired man in Poplar, Wisconsin whose vast yard is filled with voluptuous, prize-winning plants. And smack in his front yard, close to the road is an antique headboard and accompanying bed frame filled to capacity with plump pink and white annuals. A hand-lettered sign is taped to the headboard: "Yes, I am a Flower Bed."

Then there's Jerry North who lives in Glendale, Wisconsin. Jerry is tall and thin with a droopy gray mustache. (He says if his mustache is straight, he's smiling.) He, too, made a "flower bed" from an old brass headboard, footboard and a crate full of marigolds.

"I saw one in a magazine," he said.

Then he made another one, filling it with daylilies. Then someone gave him a discarded crib, which he immediately filled with sunflowers and black-eyed Susans. Then one day he snagged a wrought iron headboard from a neighbor's trash pile, carried it to his front yard and set about making yet another "flower bed" using three dozen pots of plush pink annuals. His small, square-shaped front yard was now completely covered with flower beds.

Some of the beds are even and straight, but two are placed at odd angles, which makes it difficult to maneuver a lawnmower around—these sharp angles with the narrow alleys in between. Still, Jerry manages. Maintaining them is a point of pride. But Jerry goes beyond maintaining them. That would be incredibly dull. From time to time, especially on holidays, Jerry brings out his crew of mannequins and sets them up in scenes between his flower beds and up on his porch.

HEY, I COULD MAKE A PLANTER OUT OF THAT!

"People call this house 'The Holiday House,'" Jerry says with pride. "Because I never miss one."

Locals who drive by Jerry's two-story, working-class brick house on Father's Day are greeted with an unusual sight. The mannequin he calls Xavier can be seen lounging on a chaise reading a newspaper and drinking a beer while two other mannequins, Zelda and Yvette, subserviently keep him cool by fanning him. For extra effect, he scatters empty beer cans on the ground around Xavier.

On Valentines Day, the mannequins are arranged in various embraces. All wearing red, of course.

Halloween is the best, Jerry says. He brings out the coffins he keeps stored in his garage and arranges the mannequins in and around them.

Jerry has found and been given a lot of things. Just over the fence in a garden plot set off by railroad ties lies a flat brass grave marker. His mother's grave marker.

"Oh, she's not buried there," he says. "The first one the funeral home made was cracked. So I kept it."

ABOVE *Big Bird, plucked from the flood of '97.*

RIGHT *Little Lula leads the parade in Jerry's garden party.*

Near the headstone, there is a Little Lulu doll riding a trike next to an old school desk. There are several bowling balls on stands. "Better than yard balls," Jerry says. "On St. Patrick's Day I paint eyes on them. Get it? *When Irish Eyes are Smilin'* . . ."

In the middle of Jerry's patio, next to a former carousel horse, is what's left of a black walnut tree. Jerry had the branches whacked off since the tree was overgrown and extending way beyond the top of his fence into the street. He immediately saw a new usefulness for the stubby branches. There is a bird feeder hanging from each one. And in the crotch of the tree sits a plastic *Sesame Street* Big Bird that he found floating down the street when Milwaukee experienced a flood in the spring of 1997.

Also in the backyard is a basketball hoop with wind chimes where the white cotton net used to hang. Jerry likes chimes. He says he was going to make giant chimes out of swing set poles but thought better of it. He didn't want to disturb his neighbors.

HEY, I COULD MAKE A PLANTER OUT OF THAT!

*K*ids outgrow shoes. Then a younger sister or brother gets them. After that, their moms drop them off at a Salvation Army box.

Then we grow up. Some of us Imelda Marcos wannabes simply cannot get enough footwear. We buy up all kinds of shoes. We wear our dress shoes until they go out of style. Then we either give them away or we stash them in the back of the closet until they come back in style.

But workaday shoes are worked a little harder. We pound our sneakers until the tread on their bottoms is all but gone. We wear our work books until the laces break and a hole appears in one of the soles. These shoes are in no shape to hand down to anyone. But it would be a shame to just throw them away.

Some people look at an old shoe and see, well, an old shoe. Some people see an old shoe and can't help but imagine what it would look like hanging from a tree or sitting in a garden, with it's tongue out, housing a new potted plant.

It takes vision. The trash bin is no place for something that was once so dependable.

LEFT

A Totowa, New Jersey woman saw a cemetery worker wearing this boot (and its mate) and liked it. She talked him out of both boots and gave one to her sister who made a planter out of it.

STATUES, STATUTES, AND PERSONAL STATEMENTS

W hen we think of statues, we think of Europe. Classical Greece and Rome. The Louvre in France or the castles of England and Scotland. Lots of stone and marble.

When we think of European gardens, we also think of class. Centuries-old roses and vines. And statues. Elegance, in the form of a tasteful nude statue as the focal point of a grouping of flowers. Maybe a single cherub at the foot of a walking path.

Many Europeans emigrated to America around the turn of the century. Some were rich and brought their bronze or marble garden statues with them. However, most of the immigrants, many who came to work in factories and mines, were not leaving castles or estates with sprawling gardens behind. Nonetheless, they were influenced by European traditions and sought to add a touch of elegance and "home" to the gardens they planted when they arrived.

So they placed statues in vegetable and herb gardens. For a touch of charm. In the next decade, the materials with which lawn statues and ornaments were made evolved along with

LEFT   *The proprietor of Harry's Market in Eagle River, Wisconsin, crouches by his favorite fountain statue. Harry's features a lawnful of eclectic lawn ornaments.*

ABOVE *Kissing kids . . . a concrete classic.*

RIGHT *Irene Orynycz, a high school teacher from New Wilmington, Pennsylvania, spreads mulch that smells like latte around her statues and blooms.*

mass production. Ceramic and concrete statues became popular. Animals also became more prevalent, especially in industrial towns where deer or raccoons were rarely seen.

Then came plastic—the very definition of American ingenuity and economy. In the 1930s and 40s, several companies began manufacturing plastic yard animals and "statues" that had traditionally been made of stone or concrete.

Union Products, producer of Donald Featherstone's famed pink flamingo, and several competitors crank out plastic Santas, lawn jockeys, squirrels, ducks, deer, kissing kids, and even "snomingos" (white flamingos for winter) by the thousands each year. There's no turning back. Today, these affordable bits of Americana are seen in yards everywhere: in cities, industrial towns, the suburbs and way out in the country.

They're cheap and available. It's all a matter of taste.

THE HUMBLE GNOME *Some gardeners believe they are spirits that dwell in the earth.*
Some just think they're cute. Regardless, the concrete kind are available at K-Mart for $19.99.

Basking in the Carlisle, Pennsylvania sun.

W hat is it about spraying, spewing water that is so whimsical? And who knew gargoyles had anything to do with it?

Most of us know gargoyles are medieval creations that scared away evil spirits through magic or by their sheer ugliness. Universal Statuary Corporation, which makes thousands of hand-painted gargoyles and gnomes every year, confirms that indeed, medieval artists created grand gargoyle sculptures for churches and cathedrals that were believed to ward off evil.

But a tag tied to the toe of a concrete gargoyle on sale at Builder's Square in Dania, Florida also tells us that gargoyles originally functioned as downspouts to move rainwater away from places of worship. Beyond, it tells us that they are now considered the epitome of European medieval design.

What a bonus to have something in your garden that wards off evil and spouts water, too. Gargoyles look good spilling or spitting out water. Where there is an outlandish lawn, can a silly waterfall, sprinkler or fountain be far behind? At least the water will be free of evil spirits.

ABOVE & RIGHT *Guarding the house and the delphiniums in New Wilmington, Pennsylvania.*

MOTHER GOOSE, BIKER CHICK

*L*ate on a Saturday afternoon in August, it's warm and sunny in State College, Pennsylvania just off the Penn State campus. Wholesome-looking, sunburned college kids, in town for summer school, are walking on the sidewalk in groups, carrying drinks in blue plastic cups. They are walking toward something. Anticipating.

Couples in their forties and fifties are setting up lawn chairs on patches of grass next to the curb. They look down the street to their left then look at each other. Young couples are carrying coolers and blankets and settling in for some kind of a show. Or a parade.

Then, as if out of nowhere, they come. With a slow, escalating roar, dozens of Harley Davidson motorcycles appear at the top of the hill and *vroom* down the street past the spectators. They roar by two-across or in groups of ten. The chrome on their bikes catches the sun in blinding flashes. The bikers are decked out in leather from their thick-heeled motorcycle boots to the straps on their WWI German army helmets. Harley Davidson emblems are embroidered on their jackets, even tattooed on their arms. The bikers smile and wave at the crowd that cheers as they ride past.

LEFT   *Alice Orwick with her famous goose.*

It's Hogfest weekend in State College. All the hotels in town have rows of motorcycles parked out front. Their signs are lit up with "No Vacancy" and "Welcome Bikers." Signs in restaurant windows say, "Harley Spoken Here." Bikers are welcome in town and everyone in town is welcome to temporarily become a biker.

Everyone. *Everything.* Even a cement goose that stands guard on 82-year-old Alice Orwick's front lawn.

The weekend of Hogfest, "Blessed Goose" was clad in a leather Harley jacket and a matching leather hat with goggles. She stood facing the passing bikers, her scarf blowing in the wind. They honked and gave her the thumbs-up. She just stood there in front of Alice's tidy ranch-style house with her neck stretched.

The bikers probably left town thinking the goose dresses like that every day. A true biker chick. They probably think a biker lives there, too. It is better that they left town blissfully unaware. No need for them to know that the only time Alice climbs on two wheels is when her caretaker helps her into her wheelchair. And

as for the goose: she's fickle. She changes her outfit as often as most of us change our underwear. Daily.

The goose has some thirty outfits. Every morning, someone changes Blessed Goose's clothes per Alice's direction.

If it's raining or even if it's cloudy, the fire-engine-red slicker and matching rain bonnet is the natural choice. In summer, she selects from several different bikinis, each with a little extra padding up top.

She has a luau outfit, complete with a lei and a long, brunette wig. Her gardening outfit comes out often in spring and summer. She wears her red, white and blue American flag ensemble on the Fourth of July, Flag Day, Veteran's Day and Memorial Day. Her Santa Claus outfit and pumpkin suit are worn on and around the appropriate holidays.

And as a nod to Penn State, she dresses in her Nitanny Lions cheerleader outfit during home football games and wears her graduate cap and gown at the conclusion of every school year.

Alice brought Blessed Goose back from Elyair, Ohio in 1992. Concrete geese with their own wardrobes seem to have originated in Ohio. Their popularity has spread to many neighboring states, but still, Blessed Goose is an original. She is the only concrete goose known to have an active fan club.

At least once a week, Alice receives a letter or postcard addressed to "Mother Goose," or "The Well-Dressed Goose." Sometimes the notes have a local postmark and thank her for "making my day as I drive home from work." Or a departing visitor writes after leaving town to say good-bye and compliment her on her Thanksgiving costume.

People surely seem to love her. Someone loved her so much they tried to take her late one night. But Blessed Goose is eighty-five pounds, at least. Unable to get her in the car, they fled, leaving her behind. She suffered a cracked neck in the ordeal but hey, we all have our imperfections. After all, what are scarves, leis and biker jackets with flipped-up collars for?

*A*nimal lovers are a tight-knit club. It's not unusual to see the home of a Labrador retriever owner become full of Lab books, pictures and knickknacks. What dog owner doesn't own a T-shirt with his pooch's breed pictured on the front?

And cat lovers. Need we say more? Cat mailboxes, cat slippers, cat greeting cards, and especially embroidered cat sayings in picture frames or on magnets.

It goes on. There seems to be a creeping need by animal lovers not only to be with animals but also to have an inanimate representation of their favorite beast to boot.

In the case of country folk who regularly see deer, bunnies and squirrels, statues of animals are kept as a sort of salute to these animal friends. Or, conversely, if no deer seem to ever wander into the yard, why not get a plastic one?

Of all lawn animals, geese reign supreme in animal fashion. Their only real competition for getting on Mr. Blackwell's list comes from certain dapper frogs. They needn't worry. Most of their animal contemporaries still prefer to stand yard duty in the altogether.

LEFT & ABOVE *An ode to our animal friends.*

"Using lawn ornaments to improve our surroundings is part of American culture," says Hettie Ballweber on the Internet's Master Gardener Homepage. She also calls this collection and display of non-flowering things in our yards, "a gentle mania." How apt.

The garish gardener's need to always be collecting, displaying, and rearranging may definitely be described as manic. Bertha Langren, who has a legendary outlandish lawn filled with a plastic and concrete menagerie, city Christmas ornaments and a hodgepodge of antiques says, "I'm addicted to gardening."

When is enough . . . enough? Many apologize to visitors, as Bertha Langren does, by saying, "It'll be great when I'm finished. I've got stuff you wouldn't believe. We have enough in the back and in the house to cover the whole yard."

But that is the beauty of it. Their yards are a canvas. Art in motion. Only appreciated if someone sees it. If people take part of it away with them in their minds.

These are works in progress. They will never be finished.

ABOVE *Work in progress . . . in plastic.*

RIGHT *Bertha and Marvin Langren of Minoqua, Wisconsin have found one way to avoid mowing the lawn. They've covered their front and back yard (not to mention their porch) with all manner of animals, bird houses, chimes, flags, and potted plants. They got first dibs on the huge discarded Main Street Christmas decorations from their town. They arrive early at rummage sales and flea markets to snap up old benches, swings, horseshoes, wagons, an antique grinder and fire hydrant, a US mailbox, old-fashioned bicycles, a root cutter, a cemetery basket, old washing machine tubs, a Santa's sleigh, a 14-piece Nativity scene, a milk separator, bird cages, railroad spikes, anchors, a tractor seat, an urn and a beer keg. They plant flowers in and around some of it. There's always something to move to make room for something else. Their work is never done.*

MAILBOX MARTYR

*D*on Epstein used to get his postcards, bills and frequent-flier statements by reaching into the toothy jaws of an alligator. But, no longer.

This practice came to an end when code enforcers in Coral Springs, Florida, the town where Epstein lives, decided that he should receive his mail in a "normal mailbox." Just like everyone else.

So the alligator, actually a five-foot-tall, whimsical papier-mâché alligator mailbox that Epstein made was relieved of its correspondence-receiving duties and retired to a new location alongside his house. Surely the gator sheds a crocodile tear when the mail carrier now comes by to leave letters and small parcels in the standard-issue metal mailbox that took its place.

It all began many years ago when Epstein, according to his mother, took clay he found in Bryce Canyon during a family vacation and fashioned an "Indian bowl" out of it. Then, at age twelve, Epstein won a contest at The Museum of Science and Industry in Chicago for a boat he made borrowing his mother's pink slip for a sail. His creativity was unleashed. He has been making things ever since.

LEFT *Don Epstein in the jaws of the beast.*

He says he has always been an artist, although the now-retired, 64-year-old Epstein never worked at it professionally until recently. Over the years he has worked "in the financing end" of the marine business, worked for Polaroid's fabric division and even manufactured greenhouses. He also operated women's clothing stores in Chicago. And at one time, he says, he was the top designer of artificial flowers in the country.

He switched jobs many times in his working life, but one thing remained constant: he always dabbled in drawing and sculpture, his specialty being animals and whimsical beasts. Over the years, his creatures have evolved into the truly fantastic, outlandish variety for which he has become known. And tormented.

Some time ago, Epstein, bored by his "plain old mailbox," decided to make one of his creatures into a one-of-a-kind mail receptacle.

"I knew I needed something with a big mouth," he said.

He first thought of a hippo. But then he decided it would be better to make an indigenous Florida animal, and settled on an alligator. Although he originally wanted to paint it all the colors of the rainbow, he practiced great discipline, he says, by painting the gator green (albeit different shades of lime, forest and avocado green blocked-off with a bright white stripe).

He proudly put the gator out by his curb. His mail carrier never complained about having to stick his hand deep into its mouth in order to deliver the mail. Neighbors, some whom Epstein was meeting for the first time, would stop and look. And laugh. Passersby slowed their cars and took pictures. Kids hopped off their bikes to pet the gator.

Then one day yet another visitor, this one polite but not altogether friendly, stopped by to discuss the gator. This visitor, a Planning and Zoning Department inspector acting on a complaint from an unidentified neighbor, knocked on Epstein's door and told him that his mailbox violated the law.

ABOVE *Elephant sprinkler sprays water from its trunk. Since it's not a mailbox, it gets to stay.*

LEFT *Epstein and the gator he proudly put out by his curb.*

ABOVE *Junk mail. Connecticut style.*

RIGHT *Honk! Mail call!*

Neighbors were mostly supportive of Epstein and angry at the city. One neighbor told *The Miami Herald*, "I feel good about that mailbox. Heck, some of us are talking about painting little green footprints across the street and putting up a sign that says "Gator Crossing."

It was decreed that the gator had to be removed. As a mailbox, anyway. The gator, as a purely decorative lawn ornament, has been allowed to stay.

"They can't regulate sculpture in someone's yard," Epstein says. "That's against freedom of the arts and the constitution. But they can regulate the mail."

So Epstein, who still has an elephant sprinkler on his front lawn that sprays water from its trunk, joins a very heady list of persecuted artists. He joins The Impressionists, whose work was met with howls and hoots when it was first exhibited in the late 1880s. He joins Vincent van Gogh, whose work was derided as awful and ugly and sold only one painting in his lifetime. At least Epstein can brag that he has it better than Vincent did. His sales have been brisk. In fact, he can barely keep up with the demand.

Part of the reason for the newly generated interest in his work can be attributed to Howard Alan, the man who organizes the prestigious Las Olas Arts Extravaganza in Ft. Lauderdale. Alan drove by Epstein's home one day, ironically enough, just after the zoning inspector's fateful visit. He spotted the gator, then stopped to meet Epstein and immediately made room for an exhibit of his work at his show, which was already officially closed.

"I have to have this in the show!" he said.

Of 1,000 applicants to Alan's show each year, only 250 are accepted. By the time Epstein set up his display at the show, the news stories had hit. People sought him out specifically. Ft. Lauderdale's mayor, Jim Naugle, even presented him with a key to the city.

"I had to move the gator," Epstein says. "But so many good things happened. It was really a win-win situation for me."

ABOVE *In the "Live and Let Live" Florida Keys, no one has a problem with manatees as mailboxes.*

RIGHT *Epstein's dinosaur pool fountain sculpture.*

So, like every true artist, Epstein is back to work. Not too long ago he was seen working on an enormous seven-foot dragon with long gold horns and a swirling, protruding tongue. The dragon, for which he will be paid $6,000, will function as a fountain. Like his famous gator cousin, the dragon is made of a composite of concrete and mâché resin that Epstein created.

"I wanted material that I could work with my hands, but would still stand up outdoors," he said, while painting the dragon's tongue with red acrylic.

He leaned back on his stepladder's bottom step to admire the tongue. "That's a good red," he said.

MAILBOX MARTYR

*L*ocal ordinances notwithstanding, the postal service can regulate the size and shape of mailboxes if they are determined to be unsafe for the carrier, according to Karen Schultz in the South Florida District Communications Office of the U.S. Postal Service. People are also supposed to get permission before moving a mailbox once it is installed.

Schultz, who says she would love to have a manatee mailbox (indeed, she was once photographed standing next to one), must make do with a plain mailbox as mandated by the planned Pembroke Pines, Florida, neighborhood she lives in.

"The most important thing to the post office," she says, "is the sanctity of the mail. It is a federal crime for anyone other than the carrier and the recipient to touch it."

Heady stuff for a lettuce-eating chubby water mammal who often wears a Dallas Cowboys baseball hat.

BITTERSWEET

Winters in the northern parts of the U.S. are tough. Brutal, even. Oh sure, they've got the white stuff, which is great for skiers and snowmobilers, especially at Christmas. And the lakes are frozen solid — a months-long bonus for the chosen few who list ice-fishing as a hobby on job applications. But for the majority of folks in Buffalo, New York who have to dig their cars out of two feet of snow before driving to work, winter is a chore. People in Michigan, tired of dashing from car to house through a fierce wind while struggling to balance two bags of groceries without slipping on the ice, would concur.

Summer eventually comes. Seemingly overnight, it's warm and green. The flowers are out, in vibrant, soaked-through color. The lawns are thick and cool. It stays light longer. Northern folks, especially those in the Midwest, embrace summer as if it were their fat, smiling baby grandchild. They decorate their porches with hanging plants, usually red or pink annuals potted in white plastic. They plant bright purple and white annuals in wagons pulled by little wooden donkeys and arrange them in a place of honor on the front lawn. They plant geraniums by the dozen in big, wooden barrels. In Indiana and parts of Ohio, they turn the

LEFT *John Beda of Lac du Flambeau, Wisconsin, gives some annuals a drink on the front lawn of "The Enchanted Forest," the bar he inherited. The gas pumps don't work anymore. Beda likes it just the way it is.*

ABOVE *By the Fourth of July, many people in parts of the North are bordering on giddy.*

RIGHT *Some garish gardeners go West.*

barrels on their sides and plant impatiens in the "spilled" top soil. The flowers are a greeting, a sign of the celebration of summer which begins in May and is in full bloom by June.

It continues. By the Fourth of July, many people in parts of the North are bordering on giddy. They hang American flags from their flagpoles or from stands attached to their houses. They plant red, white and blue pansies in flower beds and window boxes. People stick miniature American flags by the dozens into flower pots and flower beds.

It doesn't stop there. People take to the temporarily non-frozen ground and stick in other things. Things that spin. Things that play golf. Things that whistle or things that expand when they catch the wind. And in the trees they hang things. Windsocks. Wind chimes. Wooden Green Bay Packer guys swinging from the lowest branch.

It's all so exciting. It often gets out of hand. Garish, even. And all at once it's September and it comes to an end. The fragile plastic and wood objects are moved inside. Gone, like the vibrant annuals. It's bittersweet.

Unless . . . the celebrants move South. Many garish gardeners have brought their ornamentation tastes to newly adopted Sun Belt homes. Trailer parks outside Orlando, Florida are filled with typically northern summer garden decor such as plastic swans and spinning sunflowers. In a Tucson, Arizona mobile home retirement community, which houses many transplanted midwesterners, every other yard is garnished with reflecting balls or gnomes brought from "Up North."

Of course, local specialties are folded into the mix such as cacti with sunglasses in Arizona and lobster trap buoys strung like velvet ropes around coconut people heads in Florida.

Transplanted northerners, though inspired, by no means have a monopoly on garish gardens. Southerners have the long, sometimes endless summer to tinker in their gardens. Their results are similar. They're just less frenzied than their northern neighbors.

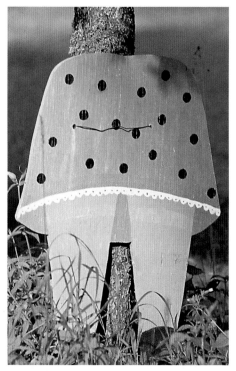

A family in Dothan, Alabama, put old tractor tires on their front lawn, painted them blue, and left them there. Weeds grew while the family mulled over what to plant inside them. Maybe they shared lemonade and talked about it. Then decided, what's the rush? Winter's a long way off. A woman in Davidson, North Carolina leaves her wooden "Bent-over Lady" out all winter. It rarely gets below freezing, she says, so why drag it in when she went to all the trouble to put her out there? After all, she did it for us. The lucky passersby.

ABOVE   *Some garish gardeners will never straighten up.*

RIGHT   *Retired tire.*

SPARE PARTS

Don't ask Todd Rumquist to go bowling. First, he doesn't bowl and second, it would be a bad idea because the temptation would be too great.

Todd, who lives in Safety Harbor, Florida with his long-time girlfriend, Kiaralinda, has some 300 bowling balls in his yard.

"I guess it started on a whim," Todd said. "We're into multiples so we put a bunch out. Then someone gave us 40 balls and it went from there."

Todd and Kiaralinda are artists. They make whimsical sculptures of animals and people. Mainly, they sell them at art festivals around the country or in the Chicago area where they spend part of every year. Often, they work on their art outside in their Florida yard where the bowling balls are both inspiration and distraction.

"People stop by and give them to us," Todd says. "Or they leave them on the doorstep. Once someone mailed one to us."

A none-too-happy mailman knocked on Todd and Kiaralinda's door one day holding a bowling ball covered with stamps.

LEFT *Todd Rumquist & Kiaralinda's Florida house . . . a must-see at Christmas.*

"I guess he thought that was going to be a regular thing," Todd said.

So far it hasn't been. But what is "regular" for this couple who has been together almost since they had the same art class in 7th grade?

In their yard, the cactuses and palm trees are surrounded by sculptures crafted from found objects and painted in bold patterns and bright colors. "The most vibrant color palette we can make," Todd says.

A palm tree is lined with bright blue bottles. Green and brown beer bottles line a flower bed. Mirrors are hung from dangling crab trap floats, painted in (what else?) bright patterns, so when the sun hits the mirrors the yard looks like a disco dance floor.

There are wood carvings and funky Plexiglas sculptures such as the fish that is in two parts so it can swim through a tree. There are multi-colored hubcaps lining a wall of the house.

And Christmas. Forget about it. The *Tampa Tribune* reported that 30,000 visitors passed by their house to see or participate in their display. Todd says some of his neighbors get a little annoyed by the traffic, but mostly, people enjoy this fun and happy place. Every year, Todd and Kiaralinda put out a donation box for charity. This year they raised $13,000 for Toys for Tots, almost entirely in one-dollar bills.

"We encourage people to participate, to stop and make an ornament," Todd says. "We want people to walk on our yard."

Christmastime or not, Todd says he doesn't mind if people stop by his house. Neighborhood kids come by and paint things, especially the bowling balls. Todd gets attached to some of them. He and Kiaralinda got especially attached to one gold metallic, fiberglass ball, which they call "G.B." (for Gold Ball). The ball has become sort of a surrogate child for them.

"It's always on my back," Todd said. "We take it everywhere."

Hence their new project, photographing and videotaping G.B. with as many people as possible.

ABOVE   *Don't ask Todd Rumquist to go bowling. Or lobster trapping.*

TOP LEFT   *On a pedestal.*

BOTTOM LEFT   *Funky fish, et al.*

The first photos were of celebrities, including swimmer Rowdy Gaines (the ball was in the water) and Michael Bolton, who they ran into during a celebrity ski weekend. They got Bob Dole to hole G.B. during a campaign parade in Illinois.

"The secret service had a fit," Todd said.

A favorite photo is of a guy from Burma (The Golden Triangle) holding the ball. The man had no idea what he was holding.

"That's what's so great about it," Todd said.

Just another day in the life of an artist who makes sculptures of people with colored telephone wires for hair (which sell for $70) and full-sized people such as a woman made entirely from kitchen parts and a man made entirely of car parts (which sell for $2,000).

Stop by anytime. Maybe Todd and Kiaralinda will be working in the yard. If not, come have a look around anyway. Leave something, take something. Just don't ask him to go bowling. The owner of the bowling alley in Safety Harbor thanks you.

ABOVE & RIGHT *A Todd & Kiaralinda original.*

SPARE PARTS